Contents

Addition

What must be added to each of these to make 100?

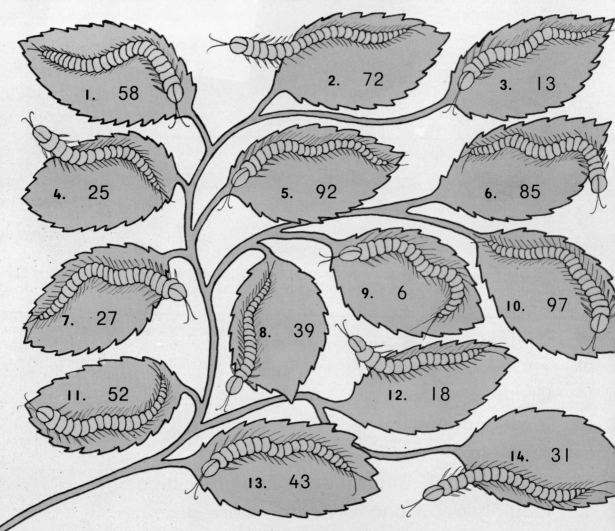

1. 58
2. 72
3. 13
4. 25
5. 92
6. 85
7. 27
8. 39
9. 6
10. 97
11. 52
12. 18
13. 43
14. 31

Add 9 to each of these numbers.

15. 16   16. 25   17. 38   18. 19   19. 53

Can you see a quick way of adding 9?

Now add 9 to each of these numbers.

20. 73   21. 49   22. 33   23. 87   24. 64

4

Add 100 to each of these numbers.

1. 14   2. 17   3. 36   4. 85   5. 92

6. 70   7. 152   8. 127   9. 160   10. 243

To add 99, add 100 and subtract 1.

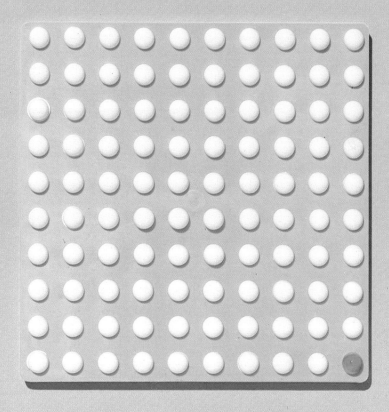

Add 99 to each of these numbers.

11. 27   12. 43   13. 87   14. 55   15. 74

16. 98   17. 121   18. 149   19. 278   20. 416

21. 372   22. 253   23. 164   24. 480   25. 722

Addition

1.
```
  3248
   127
+  247
_____
```

2.
```
   306
  2493
+   41
_____
```

3.
```
   523
    32
+ 1598
_____
```

4.
```
   602
   749
+ 3921
```

5.
```
  7248
   106
+   92
_____
```

6.
```
    49
  2368
+  322
_____
```

7.
```
   942
   725
+ 4423
_____
```

8.
```
   792
     9
+ 3978
```

9.
```
    14
  3902
+  478
_____
```

10.
```
  6923
  1413
+   78
_____
```

11.
```
  4357
   240
+ 1768
_____
```

12.
```
   323
  1478
+  492
```

13.
```
   394
   478
+ 6902
_____
```

14.
```
  7207
    84
+ 1376
_____
```

15.
```
   649
  5842
+   46
_____
```

16.
```
  3921
  4768
+   33
```

17. 4721 + 325 + 43

18. 29 + 5724 + 706

19. 804 + 93 + 4792

20. 3029 + 57 + 727

6

1.　£
　15·72
＋14·68
―――――

2.　£
　31·93
＋　0·88
―――――

3.　£
　19·17
＋　8·74
―――――

4.　£
　18·52
＋27·69
―――――

5.　£
　13·42
＋19·77
―――――

6.　£
　20·17
＋21·83
―――――

7.　£
　32·68
＋19·37
―――――

8.　£
　23·65
＋14·80
―――――

9.　£16·58 + £13·85

10.　£14·74 + £17·82

11.　m
　18·14
＋16·79
―――――

12.　m
　12·74
＋　8·87
―――――

13.　m
　10·14
＋19·98
―――――

14.　m
　6·36
＋11·29
―――――

15.　m
　7·59
＋15·68
―――――

16.　m
　13·37
＋　9·73
―――――

17.　m
　15·48
＋　6·73
―――――

18.　m
　9·72
＋12·39
―――――

19.　3·48 m + 12·72 m

20.　14·73 m + 7·29 m

7

What is missing?

What is missing here?

1.   1 5
    + 2 *
    ----
      3 8

2.   2 7
    + * 2
    ----
      5 9

3.   4 1
    + 3 *
    ----
      7 7

4.   3 3
    + * 5
    ----
      6 8

5.   2 *
    + 4 5
    ----
      6 8

6.   * 7
    + 5 1
    ----
      8 8

7.   1 *
    + 3 7
    ----
      4 9

8.   * 8
    + 4 0
    ----
      7 8

9.   4 *
    + 2 7
    ----
      7 5

10.   5 4
    + 1 *
    ----
      7 3

11.   * 9
    + 2 7
    ----
      5 6

12.   4 *
    + * 2
    ----
      8 6

British Rail ran a special train to London.
It started at Sheffield, and called at Alfreton,
Nottingham and Leicester on its way to London.
This list shows how many passengers got on at
each station.

Sheffield   185   Nottingham   230
Alfreton   86   Leicester   172

1. How many people were on the train when it
    left Alfreton?

2. How many people were on the train when it
    left Nottingham?

3. How many people went on the train to London?

4. How many more people got on the train at
    Nottingham than at Alfreton?

5. Which station had twice as many passengers as
    Alfreton?

6. The train had 720 seats.
    How many more people could have travelled on
    the train?

Length

Remember: the total distance round a shape
is called a **perimeter**.

Estimate which of these shapes has the
largest perimeter.

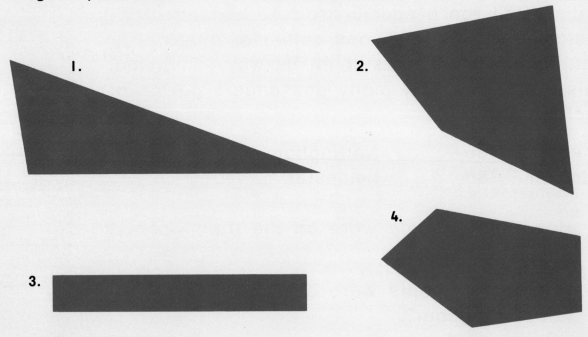

5. Measure and record the perimeter of each shape.

6. Estimate and measure the perimeter of:
   the hall;
   your desk top;
   a book;
   the playground.

Trundle wheel, bean bags

Who can throw further?

Ask a friend to help you.
Use either the hall or playground.
Make a mark on the floor.
Each throw a bean bag from the mark.
Measure the distance of each throw.
Find the difference between the length of each throw.

Do this two more times.

11

Length

1. m
    4·32
    ×   7
    ─────

    ─────

2. m
    2·95
    ×   5
    ─────

    ─────

3. m
    5·09
    ×   6
    ─────

    ─────

4. m
    1·78
    ×   9
    ─────

    ─────

5. m
    6·17
    ×   4
    ─────

    ─────

6. m
    3·43
    ×   3
    ─────

    ─────

7. m
    5·64
    ×   7
    ─────

    ─────

8. m
    4·71
    ×   5
    ─────

    ─────

9. m
    5)1·50

10. m
    3)4·26

11. m
    6)9·24

12. m
    6)8·94

13. m
    4)0·96

14. m
    5)6·80

15. m
    10)5·50

16. m
    3)1·26

. Mr. Timson's garage is 7 m long.
His car is 4·75 m long.
His trailer is 1·65 m long.
How much room is there to spare?

.. Mr. Spencer, the shopkeeper, stacked 5 boxes on top
of each other.
Each box was 0·75 m high.
How high was the stack of boxes?

.. Mr. Richards built a fence.
It had 6 panels.
Each panel was 1·28 m long.
How long was the fence?

. Mr. Smith's fence, next door, had 9 panels.
Each panel of his fence was 1·19 m long.
How much longer was his fence than Mr. Richards'?

. The captain of the ferry takes on board 8 cars.
Each car needs 3·84 m.
What is the total length needed by the cars?

Subtraction

Take 9 from each of these:

1. 78		2. 236		3. 678		4. 376	
5. 480		6. 219		7. 105		8. 306	
9. 204		10. 408		11. 1007		12. 2003	

Take 100 from each of these:

13. 327	14. 963	15. 2741	16. 3803
17. 4962	18. 8713	19. 1003	20. 3064
21. 5029	22. 3081	23. 4080	24. 1072

Subtract 99 from each of these:

25. 106	26. 348	27. 273	28. 1245
29. 1372	30. 2413	31. 3428	32. 1638

There is a quick way of subtracting 99.
Subtract 100 and then add 1.

Use the quick way to subtract 99 from these.

33. 647	34. 830	35. 2175	36. 3178
37. 6943	38. 2706	39. 1048	40. 2073
41. 4081	42. 7029	43. 8081	44. 1072
45. 5302	46. 3092	47. 7380	48. 2167

1. 3478
    − 259
    ‾‾‾‾‾‾‾

2. 3809
    − 1423
    ‾‾‾‾‾‾‾

3. 5386
    − 640
    ‾‾‾‾‾‾‾

4. 6430
    − 1163
    ‾‾‾‾‾‾‾

5. 5634
    − 1864
    ‾‾‾‾‾‾‾

6. 3576
    − 689
    ‾‾‾‾‾‾‾

7. 4300
    − 1162
    ‾‾‾‾‾‾‾

8. 3068
    − 395
    ‾‾‾‾‾‾‾

9. 7000
    − 3647
    ‾‾‾‾‾‾‾

10. 5036
    − 2178
    ‾‾‾‾‾‾‾

11. 5603
    − 835
    ‾‾‾‾‾‾‾

12. 7324
    − 5104
    ‾‾‾‾‾‾‾

13. 3200
    − 1742
    ‾‾‾‾‾‾‾

14. 6003
    − 4218
    ‾‾‾‾‾‾‾

15. 3604
    − 428
    ‾‾‾‾‾‾‾

16. 7362
    − 5187
    ‾‾‾‾‾‾‾

17. 8007
    − 4132
    ‾‾‾‾‾‾‾

18. 4000
    − 2635
    ‾‾‾‾‾‾‾

19. 4307
    − 2549
    ‾‾‾‾‾‾‾

20. 7000
    − 4360
    ‾‾‾‾‾‾‾

21. 6285
    − 436
    ‾‾‾‾‾‾‾

22. 7032
    − 3124
    ‾‾‾‾‾‾‾

23. 2831
    − 648
    ‾‾‾‾‾‾‾

24. 2520
    − 1618
    ‾‾‾‾‾‾‾

Subtraction

1.
$$
\begin{array}{r}
3642 \\
-\ 684 \\
\hline
\end{array}
$$

2.
$$
\begin{array}{r}
3792 \\
-\ 1834 \\
\hline
\end{array}
$$

3.
$$
\begin{array}{r}
6417 \\
-\ 4235 \\
\hline
\end{array}
$$

4.
$$
\begin{array}{r}
7000 \\
-\ 4123 \\
\hline
\end{array}
$$

5. g
$$
\begin{array}{r}
430 \\
-\ 246 \\
\hline
\end{array}
$$

6. g
$$
\begin{array}{r}
654 \\
-\ 246 \\
\hline
\end{array}
$$

7. g
$$
\begin{array}{r}
364 \\
-\ 185 \\
\hline
\end{array}
$$

8. g
$$
\begin{array}{r}
540 \\
-\ 472 \\
\hline
\end{array}
$$

9. £
$$
\begin{array}{r}
8 \cdot 60 \\
-\ 4 \cdot 27 \\
\hline
\end{array}
$$

10. £
$$
\begin{array}{r}
5 \cdot 08 \\
-\ 1 \cdot 39 \\
\hline
\end{array}
$$

11. £
$$
\begin{array}{r}
6 \cdot 00 \\
-\ 2 \cdot 25 \\
\hline
\end{array}
$$

12. £
$$
\begin{array}{r}
4 \cdot 33 \\
-\ 1 \cdot 64 \\
\hline
\end{array}
$$

13. £
$$
\begin{array}{r}
3 \cdot 46 \\
-\ 1 \cdot 80 \\
\hline
\end{array}
$$

14. £
$$
\begin{array}{r}
4 \cdot 25 \\
-\ 1 \cdot 77 \\
\hline
\end{array}
$$

15. £
$$
\begin{array}{r}
3 \cdot 08 \\
-\ 1 \cdot 69 \\
\hline
\end{array}
$$

16. £
$$
\begin{array}{r}
5 \cdot 00 \\
-\ 3 \cdot 64 \\
\hline
\end{array}
$$

17. m
$$
\begin{array}{r}
7 \cdot 50 \\
-\ 4 \cdot 75 \\
\hline
\end{array}
$$

18. m
$$
\begin{array}{r}
3 \cdot 27 \\
-\ 1 \cdot 96 \\
\hline
\end{array}
$$

19. m
$$
\begin{array}{r}
3 \cdot 55 \\
-\ 1 \cdot 78 \\
\hline
\end{array}
$$

20. m
$$
\begin{array}{r}
4 \cdot 06 \\
-\ 2 \cdot 39 \\
\hline
\end{array}
$$

What must be added to these numbers to make 100?

1. 35   2. 42   3. 70   4. 51

5. 73   6. 68   7. 14   8. 86

9. 27   10. 49   11. 93   12. 46

How much change will be given?

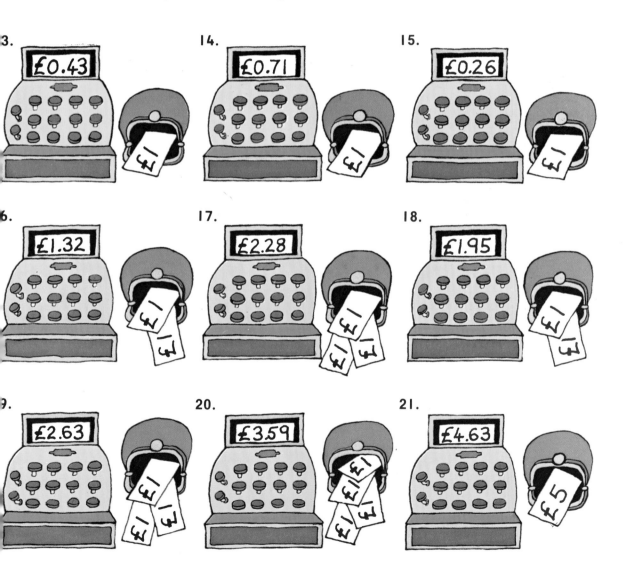

1. Mr. Randall bought a tin of paint costing £3·64.
   What change did he get from £5?

2. Jenny has saved £8·28.
   She wants to save £10 altogether.
   How much more does she need to save?

3. John is 1·58 m tall.
   Dino is 1·70 m tall.
   How much taller is Dino than John?

4. A roll of cloth is 25 m long.
   10·60 m have been cut off.
   How much is left on the roll?

5. In a leap year 147 days have passed.
   How many days are left?

6. I bought two records costing £3·75 each.
   How much change did I get from £10?

7. Mrs. Patel has 750 g of sugar in her sugar bag.
   She fills the sugar basin with 483 g of sugar.
   What is the weight of the sugar left in the bag?

8. A shelf is to be fixed into a space 1·23 m long.
   Ron has a piece of wood 2 m long.
   How much must be cut off the wood?

Mr. Jennings built a garage. He ordered 4500 bricks.

1. He used 980 bricks in the base.
    How many bricks did he have left?

2. He used 3454 bricks to build the rest of the garage.
    How many bricks did he have left?

3. He bought 800 tiles for the roof.
    The firm only delivered 648 tiles.
    How many was he short?

4. He borrowed £1200 from the bank to pay for the garage.
    It cost £2074 to build.
    How much more money did he need?

5. The wood on the garage cost £306.
    The concrete cost £76.
    What did the rest of the building materials cost?

19

Shape

Plane shapes

Remember: ≫ This means copy into your book.

A shape with 5 straight sides
is called a **pentagon**.

Find a pentagon.
Draw round it.

≫ This is a pentagon.

A shape with 8 straight sides
is called an **octagon**.

Find an octagon.
Draw round it.

≫ This is an octagon.

A shape with 3 equal sides
is called an **equilateral triangle**.

Find an equilateral triangle.
Draw round it.

≫ This is an equilateral triangle.

1. An equilateral triangle has ☐ vertices.

2. A _____ has 5 vertices.

3. An octagon has ☐ vertices.

20

Plane shapes, 16 pin geo-board, spotty paper

All shapes with 4 sides and 4 vertices are called
quadrilaterals.

Find some quadrilaterals.
Draw round them.
Make 3 different quadrilaterals on the geo-board.
Draw them on spotty paper.
Stick the paper in your book.

» All these shapes are quadrilaterals.

Plane shapes, plain paper

Draw round a circle on plain paper.
Cut it out and fold it in half.

Open the circle.
The fold is called a **diameter**.
Fold it again to make another
diameter.
Stick the circle in your book.

≫ The folds are called diameters.

A diameter cuts a circle in half.
Half a circle is called
a **semi-circle**.

This pattern is made of semi-circles.
Make your own pattern with semi-circles.

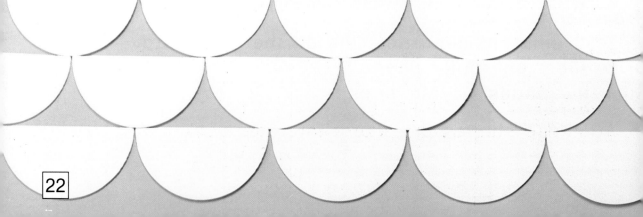

Plane shapes

Draw round a rectangle.
Draw a straight line between two vertices.

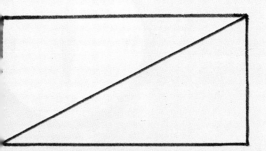

≫ A straight line between two vertices is called a **diagonal**.

Draw round a square.
Draw two diagonals on your square.

≫ The square has 2 diagonals.

Draw round a pentagon.
Draw as many diagonals as you can.

. ≫ The pentagon has ☐ diagonals.

Do the same with a hexagon.

. ≫ The hexagon has ☐ diagonals.

. Which shape with vertices has no diagonals?

. Measure the diagonal distance of:
your exercise book; your desk; this book.

Angles

Compass, plane shapes, plain paper

Ask your teacher to show you which end
of the needle points to north.

Take the compass to the centre of
the playground.
Make the north needle point to the letter N.
Write what you see when you look
north, east, south and west.

Draw round a circle on plain paper.
Cut it out.
Fold it like this:

Open the circle and label it like this:

Stick the circle in your book.

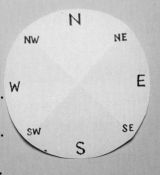

1. NE means _____ .

2. SE means _____ .

3. SW means _____ .

4. NW means _____ .

Plain paper

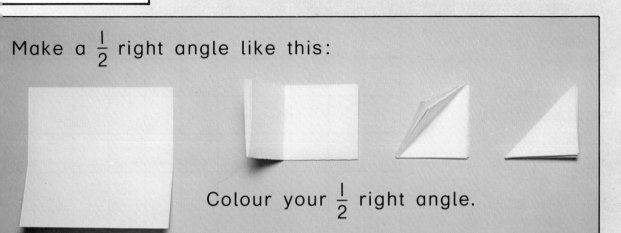

Make a $\frac{1}{2}$ right angle like this:

Colour your $\frac{1}{2}$ right angle.

Use your $\frac{1}{2}$ right angle to find if these angles are:

less than $\frac{1}{2}$ right angle;

greater than $\frac{1}{2}$ right angle;

or $\frac{1}{2}$ right angle.

Multiplication

Copy this table on squared paper. It is called a **table square**. Complete it.

×	1	2	3	4	5	6	7	8	9	10
1										
2				8						
3										
4										
5							35			
6										
7										
8		16								
9										
10										

1.   128
    ×   5
    _____

2.   209
    ×   4
    _____

3.   117
    ×   3
    _____

4.   108
    ×   8
    _____

5.   421
    ×   7
    _____

6.   380
    ×   6
    _____

7.   594
    ×   10
    _____

8.   286
    ×   9
    _____

Set these out in the easiest way before doing them.

1. 264 × 7   2. £1·03 × 5   3. £2·48 × 6

4. 293 × 8   5. 252 × 4   6. £3·87 × 3

7. 175 × 10   8. 503 × 2   9. £1·20 × 9

10. 362 × 7   11. 401 × 10   12. 199 × 6

13. £3·29 × 4   14. 506 × 8   15. £1·06 × 7

16. £7·18 × 6   17. 207 × 5   18. £4·90 × 8

19. 369 × 9   20. £2·71 × 10   21. 309 × 3

Multiply each of the these numbers by 10.

22. 24   23. 36   24. 89   25. 104

26. 232   27. 169   28. 426   29. 383

30. 880   31. 487   32. 719   33. 69

Look at each answer and the number you started with.
Can you see a quick way of multiplying by 10?
Test it with 5 more numbers.

Multiply each of these numbers by 10.

34. 103   35. 264   36. 97   37. 132

38. 461   39. 100   40. 206   41. 348

If we multiply 2 by 5 we get 10.
We say that 2 and 5 are **factors** of 10.
If we multiply 1 by 10 we get 10.
We can show factors like this:

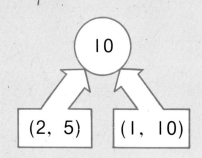

The factors of 10 are 1, 2, 5, 10.

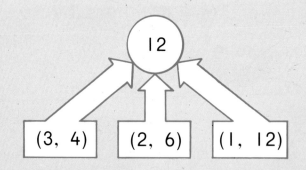

The factors of 12 are 1, 2, 3, 4, 6, 12.

Find the factors of these numbers.
Write them in the same way.

1. 8	2. 15	3. 30	4. 21	5. 27
6. 24	7. 16	8. 36	9. 18	10. 40
11. 32	12. 9	13. 48	14. 20	15. 14

1. $\begin{array}{r} 1121 \\ \times \quad 7 \\ \hline \\ \hline \end{array}$

2. $\begin{array}{r} 1036 \\ \times \quad 8 \\ \hline \\ \hline \end{array}$

3. $\begin{array}{r} 2178 \\ \times \quad 2 \\ \hline \\ \hline \end{array}$

4. $\begin{array}{r} 1129 \\ \times \quad 3 \\ \hline \\ \hline \end{array}$

5. $\begin{array}{r} 1366 \\ \times \quad 6 \\ \hline \\ \hline \end{array}$

6. $\begin{array}{r} 1370 \\ \times \quad 7 \\ \hline \\ \hline \end{array}$

7. $\begin{array}{r} 2499 \\ \times \quad 3 \\ \hline \\ \hline \end{array}$

8. $\begin{array}{r} 3097 \\ \times \quad 3 \\ \hline \\ \hline \end{array}$

9. $\begin{array}{r} 1364 \\ \times \quad 5 \\ \hline \\ \hline \end{array}$

10. $\begin{array}{r} 947 \\ \times \quad 10 \\ \hline \\ \hline \end{array}$

11. $\begin{array}{r} 963 \\ \times \quad 9 \\ \hline \\ \hline \end{array}$

12. $\begin{array}{r} 1426 \\ \times \quad 5 \\ \hline \\ \hline \end{array}$

13. $\begin{array}{r} 1872 \\ \times \quad 4 \\ \hline \\ \hline \end{array}$

14. $\begin{array}{r} 2963 \\ \times \quad 2 \\ \hline \\ \hline \end{array}$

15. $\begin{array}{r} 1038 \\ \times \quad 7 \\ \hline \\ \hline \end{array}$

16. $\begin{array}{r} 1192 \\ \times \quad 6 \\ \hline \\ \hline \end{array}$

17. $\begin{array}{r} 1761 \\ \times \quad 5 \\ \hline \\ \hline \end{array}$

18. $\begin{array}{r} 1387 \\ \times \quad 6 \\ \hline \\ \hline \end{array}$

19. $\begin{array}{r} 1096 \\ \times \quad 9 \\ \hline \\ \hline \end{array}$

20. $\begin{array}{r} 1229 \\ \times \quad 8 \\ \hline \\ \hline \end{array}$

21. $\begin{array}{r} 1638 \\ \times \quad 6 \\ \hline \\ \hline \end{array}$

22. $\begin{array}{r} 1495 \\ \times \quad 4 \\ \hline \\ \hline \end{array}$

23. $\begin{array}{r} 401 \\ \times \quad 10 \\ \hline \\ \hline \end{array}$

24. $\begin{array}{r} 1416 \\ \times \quad 3 \\ \hline \\ \hline \end{array}$

29

Capacity

Remember: 1000 ml = 1 litre

	ml
One jug holds	720
The other jug holds	830
Total	1550

1550 ml = 1 l 550 ml

1.

	ml
One jug holds	560
The other jug holds	780
Total	

[   ] ml = [ ] l [   ] ml

2.

	ml
One bottle holds	470
The other bottle holds	650
Total	

[   ] ml = [ ] l [   ] ml

A short way of writing 1 l 550 ml is 1·550 l.
Write these in the short way.

1. 1 l 480 ml   2. 1 l 700 ml   3. 2 l 550 ml

4. 1 l 235 ml   5. 2 l 990 ml   6. 3 l 520 ml

	ml
One bottle holds	480
The other bottle holds	740
Total	1220

1220 ml = 1·220 l

Find the total of each of these.
Write the answer in the short way.

7. A vase that holds 750 ml
and another that holds 390 ml.

8. A glass that holds 275 ml
and another that holds 870 ml.

9. A jug that holds 920 ml
and another that holds 470 ml.

10. A kettle that holds 680 ml
and another that holds 655 ml.

11. A container that holds 805 ml
and another that holds 795 ml.

31

Fractions

5 gummed paper circles

1. Fold and cut the circle in half.

2. Fold one half in half. Cut along the fold.

3. Fold one quarter in half. Cut along the fold. Each piece is called an **eighth**.
We write an eighth like this: $\frac{1}{8}$

4. Stick the pieces in your book. Label them like this:

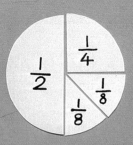

Fold and cut a circle into quarters. Label each piece $\frac{1}{4}$

Fold and cut a circle into eighths. Label each piece $\frac{1}{8}$.

Stick the shapes in your book like this:

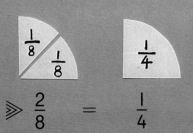

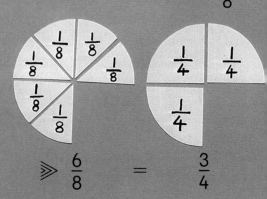

$\gg \frac{2}{8} = \frac{1}{4}$

$\gg \frac{6}{8} = \frac{3}{4}$

32

Fold and cut a circle in half. Label each piece $\frac{1}{2}$.

Fold and cut a circle into eighths. Label each piece $\frac{1}{8}$.

Stick the shapes in your book like this:

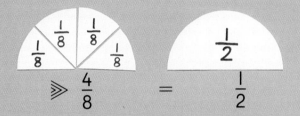

What fraction is coloured?

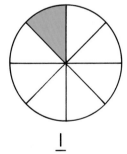

$\frac{1}{8}$

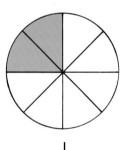

$\frac{1}{4}$

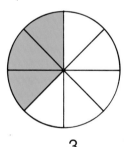

$\frac{3}{8}$

1.

$?$

2.

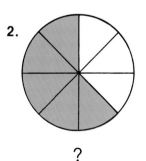

$?$

3.

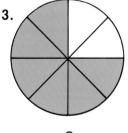

$?$

4.

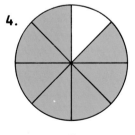

$?$

5.

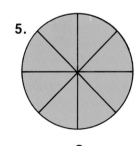

$?$

This is one of Richard's chocolate bars.
It has 8 pieces.

Each piece is $\frac{1}{8}$ of the bar.

Richard breaks his chocolate bar into parts.
What fraction of a bar is each part?

1.

$\frac{1}{2}$ or $\frac{\square}{8}$

2.

$\frac{4}{8}$ or $\frac{\square}{2}$

3.

$\frac{2}{8}$ or $\frac{1}{\square}$

4.

$\frac{6}{8}$ or $\frac{\square}{4}$

Complete these:

1. $\frac{4}{8}$ is the same as ☐   2. $\frac{3}{4}$ is the same as ☐

3. $\frac{2}{8}$ is the same as ☐   4. $\frac{1}{2}$ is the same as ☐

5. $\frac{1}{4}$ is the same as ☐   6. $\frac{6}{8}$ is the same as ☐

What fraction of each shape is coloured?
What fraction of each shape is not coloured?

7.

8.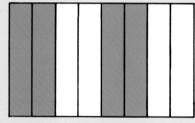

9.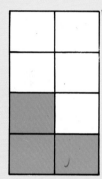

10.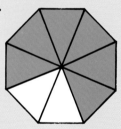

11.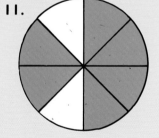

12.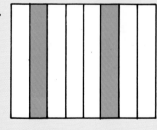

13.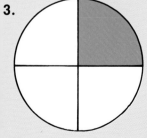

14.

35

Fractions

Squared paper

Draw these shapes on squared paper.
What fraction of each shape is coloured?

1. Colour $\frac{1}{4}$ blue.

   Colour $\frac{1}{2}$ red.

2. Colour $\frac{3}{4}$ blue.

   Colour $\frac{1}{8}$ red.

3. Colour $\frac{3}{8}$ red.

   Colour $\frac{1}{8}$ blue.

4. Colour $\frac{1}{4}$ blue.

   Colour $\frac{1}{8}$ red.

5. Colour $\frac{3}{8}$ blue.

   Colour $\frac{3}{8}$ red.

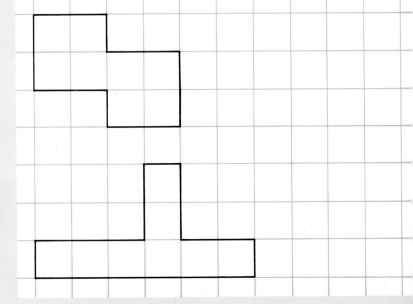

> To find $\frac{1}{8}$ of a quantity, divide by 8.

Find:

1. $\frac{1}{8}$ of 496   2. $\frac{1}{8}$ of 176   3. $\frac{1}{8}$ of 808

4. $\frac{1}{4}$ of 624   5. $\frac{1}{3}$ of 813   6. $\frac{1}{2}$ of 750

7. $\frac{1}{8}$ of 240   8. $\frac{1}{2}$ of 620   9. $\frac{1}{3}$ of 402

10. Tony has 64 picture cards of footballers.

    David only has $\frac{1}{4}$ as many.

    How many does David have?

11. Jason counted 96 cars passing his house.

    His sister Debbie counted $\frac{1}{8}$ as many buses.

    How many buses went past?

12. Mr. Johnson planted 108 cabbages in his garden.

    Mr. Evans, next door, planted only $\frac{1}{3}$ as many.

    How many cabbages did Mr. Evans plant?

13. The cricket captain scored 142 runs in the cricket match.
    The rest of the team only scored $\frac{1}{2}$ as many altogether.
    How many runs did the whole team score?

Weight

> Weights, balance, set of weighing objects,
> bathroom scales

Find the kilogram weight.
Balance the kilogram weight with 500 g weights.

> ≫ I kilogram = ☐ grams
> ≫ I kg = ☐ g

Find several objects which weigh about one
kilogram.
Estimate what each object weighs.
Record your estimates in a list like this:

Less than I kg	About I kg	More than I kg

Now use your balance and kg weight to find
if you were correct.

Bathroom scales weigh in kg. Weigh yourself.
Estimate the weight of six people in
your class. Weigh them.
Record your results in a list.

Name	Estimate	Weight

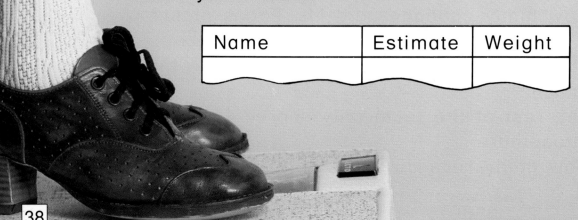

Remember: 1000 g = 1 kg

If an answer comes to more than 1 kg we can write it
like this: 650 g +   730 g = 1380 g
                              1380 g = 1 kg 380 g

Do these in the same way.

1.   700 g + 560 g   2.   540 g + 760 g

3.   480 g + 940 g   4.   370 g + 980 g

5.   630 g + 730 g   6.   820 g + 390 g

A short way of writing 1 kg 380 g is 1·380 kg.
Write these weights in the short way.

7.
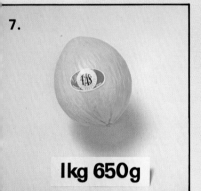
1kg 650g

8.

4kg 630g

9.

2kg 500g

10.
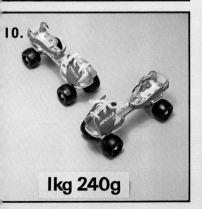
1kg 240g

11.
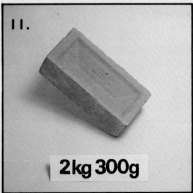
2kg 300g

12.

3kg 490g

Division

Complete these:

1.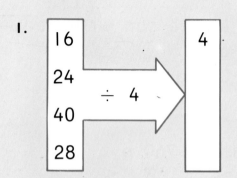

2.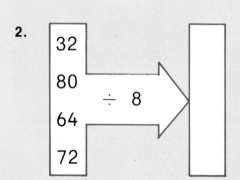

3. 4)404 **4.** 8)328 **5.** 5)735 **6.** 6)834

7. 10)620 **8.** 9)783 **9.** 7)973 **10.** 8)696

11. 4)364 **12.** 8)720 **13.** 7)637 **14.** 10)730

15. 9)810 **16.** 5)490 **17.** 6)606 **18.** 8)968

19. How many 9s in 468? **20.** Find $\frac{1}{3}$ of 726.

21. 672 ÷ 8 **22.** Find $\frac{1}{2}$ of 126.

23. Find $\frac{1}{4}$ of 204. **24.** Find $\frac{1}{3}$ of 213.

25. Share 125 marbles equally among 5 children.

have 47 sweets to share among 5 children.
Each child has 9 sweets, and there are 2 left over.
Those left over are called the **remainder**.
A short way of writing remainder is **r**.

$$5 \overline{)47} \quad 9 \, r \, 2$$

Work these out in the same way.

1. $8 \overline{)66}$ 2. $4 \overline{)95}$ 3. $2 \overline{)73}$ 4. $5 \overline{)116}$

5. $3 \overline{)263}$ 6. $8 \overline{)620}$ 7. $6 \overline{)724}$ 8. $7 \overline{)813}$

9. $9 \overline{)572}$ 10. $10 \overline{)473}$ 11. $8 \overline{)298}$ 12. $7 \overline{)493}$

13. $7 \overline{)605}$ 14. $10 \overline{)592}$ 15. $5 \overline{)486}$ 16. $8 \overline{)641}$

How many are left over if I share:

17. 496 stamps equally among 7 children?

18. 324 toy soldiers equally among 10 children?

Division

Divide each of these numbers by 10.

1. 60	2. 240	3. 380	4. 500	5. 630
6. 721	7. 427	8. 368	9. 932	10. 440

Look at each of your answers, and the number you started with.
Can you see a quick way of dividing by 10?
Test it with 5 more numbers.

Divide each of these numbers by 10.

11. 310	12. 870	13. 430	14. 205	15. 372
16. 296	17. 108	18. 700	19. 639	20. 547

21. A bookcase holding 270 books, has 10 shelves.
Each shelf has the same number of books.
How many books are on each shelf?

22. A farmer had 740 sheep spread equally among
10 fields.
How many sheep were in each field?

Some of these have remainders.

1. $3\overline{)3729}$ 2. $5\overline{)4720}$ 3. $8\overline{)5680}$

4. $9\overline{)3972}$ 5. $10\overline{)4600}$ 6. $7\overline{)6376}$

7. $8\overline{)9346}$ 8. $6\overline{)7322}$ 9. $5\overline{)8731}$

10. $4\overline{)964}$ 11. $2\overline{)9362}$ 12. $10\overline{)879}$

13. $7\overline{)9212}$ 14. $8\overline{)6862}$ 15. $6\overline{)4921}$

16. $7\overline{)899}$ 17. $5\overline{)6436}$ 18. $9\overline{)1901}$

19. Three pirates shared 471 bars of gold equally.
    How many did each get?

20. James shared 125 conkers equally among himself
    and his three friends.
    How many did each have?
    How many were left over?

21. A school has 256 children.
    They are divided equally among 8 classes.
    How many children are in each class?

Area

Find how many squares there are in each of these shapes.

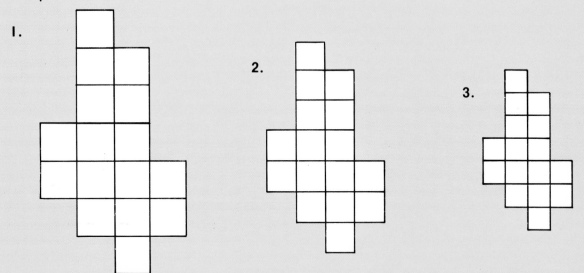

1.

2.

3.

These shapes have the same number of squares.
But you can see they are different sizes.
When finding areas we need the same sized square for each shape.

This is a I cm square

Its area is I **square centimetre**.
We write it like this: I **cm²**.

The area of this shape is 7 cm².

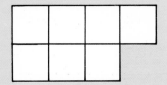

Find the areas of these shapes.

1.

2.

3.

4.

5.

6.

Transparent cm squared grid

Look at each object.
Estimate its area.
Find its area using the transparent grid.
Record your results in a list.

Object	Estimate	Area

1.

2.

3.

4.

5.

6.

7.

8.

10.

9.

12.

11.

Money

1. £
   2·75
   + 1·37
   ———

2. £
   3·68
   + 2·95
   ———

3. £
   7·20
   − 4·96
   ———

4. £
   8·40
   − 3·95
   ———

5. £
   2·35
   ×   4
   ———

6. £
   2·08
   ×   6
   ———

7. £
   1·57
   ×   9
   ———

8. £
   2·48
   ×   8
   ———

9. £
   5) 6·35

10. £
    8) 9·12

11. £
    7) 6·44

12. £
    6) 8·3

13. £
    4) 9·72

14. £
    10) 8·70

15. £
    9) 7·74

16. £
    7) 8·7

17. How much more money is £7·45 than £3·58?

18. What is the total of £3·73, £2·97, and £5·39?

19. Divide £2·52 by 3.

20. How much change do I get from £5 if I spend £2·50 on a book and 65p on a magazine?

	York	Skegness	Blackpool
Adult	£3·60	£2·80	£3·45
Child under 14	£2·40	£1·90	£2·55

. Mr. Taylor has 4 children, all under 14.
He decided to take his wife and children to York.
How much did it cost him?

. Mr. Selby has 3 children, aged 16, 10 and 9.
He decided to take his wife and children to
Blackpool.
How much did it cost him?

. Mrs. Martin has 3 children under 14.
Her neighbour has 3 children under 14 as well.
Mrs. Martin took the 6 children to Skegness.
How much did it cost her?

. Choose one of the trips for your family to go on.
How much will it cost?

Mr. Jones wants to start a football team.
How much will it cost him to buy:

1. 3 footballs?
2. 10 footballer's outfits?
3. 2 goalkeeper's outfits?
4. 4 corner flags?
5. 2 sets of goalposts?
6. 2 sets of goal nets?

7. How much will it cost him altogether?

Footballs @ £8·75 each
Corner flags @ £1·85 each
Footballer's outfits @ £5·85 each
Goalkeeper's outfits @ £5·85 each
Set of junior goalposts @ £9·70 each
Goal nets @ £4·30 each

Mrs. Jones wants to start a netball team.
How much will it cost her to buy:

1. 2 netballs?
2. 7 netball skirts?
3. 7 netball blouses?
4. 2 netball posts?
5. 7 pairs of plimsolls?
6. 7 pairs of socks?

7. How much will it cost her altogether?

Netballs @ £3·90 each
Netball skirts @ £6·75 each
Netball blouses @ £4·15 each
Netball posts @ £8·70 each
Plimsolls @ £1·99 a pair
White socks @ 85p a pair

Time

 This clock shows 6.05.

We call it 5 past 6.

 This clock shows 6.10.

We call it 10 past 6.

 This clock shows 6.20.

We call it 20 past 6.

 This clock shows 6.25.

We call it 25 past 6.

Copy this into your book.

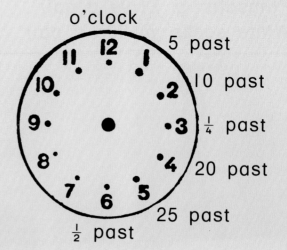

Stamp 6 clock faces.
Show these times.
Write the time under each clock.

1. 5 past 3
2. 10 past 6
3. $\frac{1}{4}$ past 7

4. 20 past 5
5. $\frac{1}{2}$ past 9
6. 25 past 4

52

 This clock shows 6.35.

We call it 25 to 7.

 This clock shows 6.40.

We call it 20 to 7.

 This clock shows 6.50.

We call it 10 to 7.

 This clock shows 6.55.

We call it 5 to 7.

Copy this into your book.

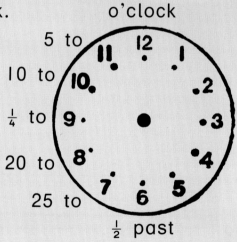

Stamp 6 clock faces.
Show these times.
Write the time under each clock.

1. $\frac{1}{2}$ past 3   2. 25 to 8   3. $\frac{1}{4}$ to 3

4. 5 to 6   5. 10 to 4   6. 20 to 6

Graphs

John's older brother is a train spotter.
He counted the number of trains passing through
Ambergate one afternoon.
This graph shows what he found.

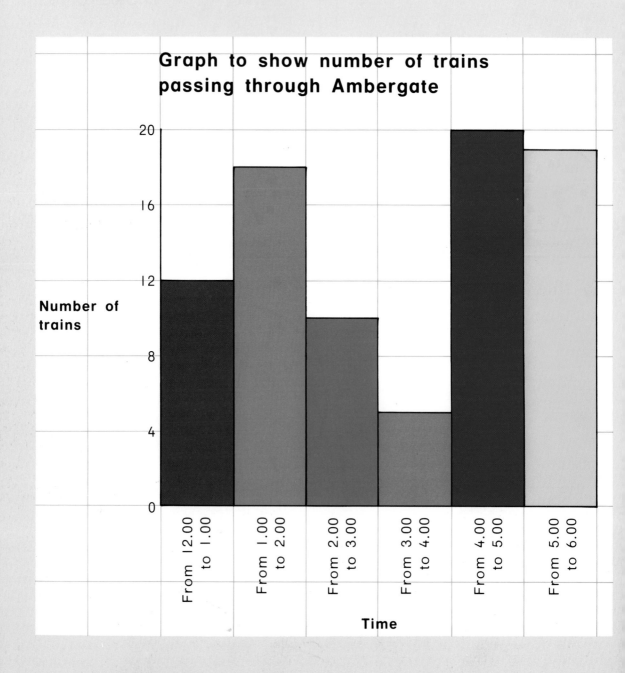

Graph to show number of trains passing through Ambergate

Number of trains

Time

The vertical axis on this graph goes up in 4s.
Each square is worth 4.
1. What is half a square worth?
2. What is quarter of a square worth?
3. What is three-quarters of a square worth?

Answer these questions from the graph.

4. Which hour had most trains?
5. Which hour had the fewest trains?
6. How many trains passed through at the busiest hour?
7. How many trains passed through from 12.00 to 1.00?
8. How many trains passed through from 5.00 to 6.00?
9. Which hour had half as many trains as the busiest hour?
10. How many trains altogether passed through Ambergate that afternoon?

John's mother works in a clothes shop.
She had to count how many clothes were in the shop.
This is what she found.

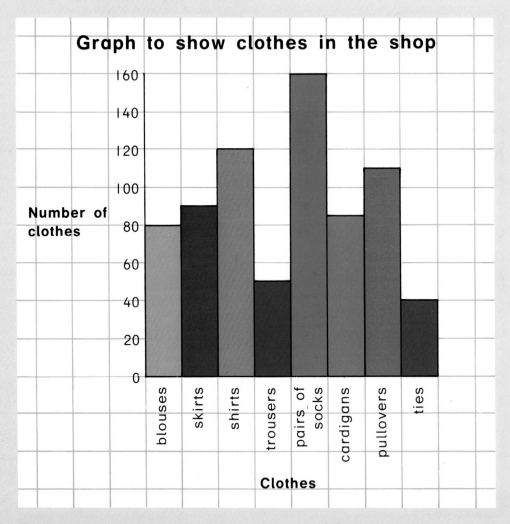

The vertical axis goes up in 20s.

1. What is half a square worth?
2. What is quarter of a square worth?
3. What is three-quarters of a square worth?
4. Make a table to show how many of each sort of clothes were in the shop.

John's local football team is Belper Villa.
He goes with his brother and sister to watch them play.
John's father goes as well.
This table shows approximately how many people watch
the matches.

Matches	Ist	2nd	3rd	4th	5th	6th
Number of people	700	550	800	950	400	800

Draw a graph to show this information.
Make your vertical axis go up in 100s.
Each square is worth 100;
so half a square is worth 50.

57

Investigations

0   I   2   3   4   5   6   7   8   9

These are **digits**.
56 is a two digit number containing the digits 5 and 6.
247 is a three digit number containing the digits
2, 4 and 7.

Write down any three digit number. The first digit must be at least 2 greater than the last digit.	7 3 2
Reverse the order of the digits.	− 2 3 7
Find the difference between the two numbers.	4 9 5
Reverse the order of the digits.	+ 5 9 4
Add the two numbers.	1 0 8 9

Here is another example: 5 I 2

                − 2 I 5   Reverse the digits
                —————   and subtract.
                   2 9 7
                + 7 9 2   Reverse the digits
                —————   and add.
                I 0 8 9

Investigate with other three digit numbers.
What do you notice?

To find the digital sum of any number add the digits together.

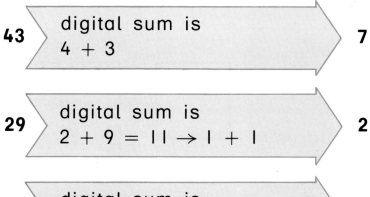

43 > digital sum is
4 + 3 > **7**

29 > digital sum is
2 + 9 = 11 → 1 + 1 > **2**

121 > digital sum is
1 + 2 + 1 > **4**

The digital sum of the three times table is:

1 × 3 = 3   digital sum   3

2 × 3 = 6   6

3 × 3 = 9   9

4 × 3 = 12   3

5 × 3 = 15   6

6 × 3 = 18   9

7 × 3 = 21   3

8 × 3 = 24   6   Find the digital sum
                                  of other tables.
9 × 3 = 27   9   Do they always make

0 × 3 = 30   3   a pattern?

Squared paper, isometric paper, pegboard, pegs

Use squared paper.
Draw a pattern of squares
increasing in size like this:

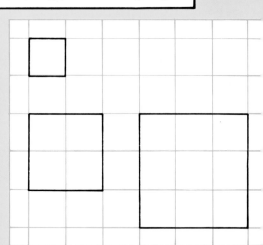

Continue the pattern until you
have drawn 6 squares.
Write how many small squares
there are in each square.

Use isometric paper.
Draw a pattern of triangles
increasing in size like this:

Continue the pattern until you
have drawn 7 triangles.
Write how many small triangles
there are in each triangle.

Use the pegboard.
Make a pattern of squares
increasing in size like this:

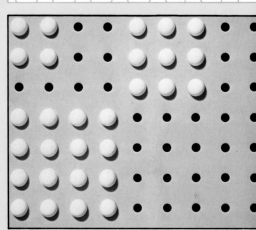

Continue as far as you can.
Write how many pegs there
are in each square.

Use the pegboard.
Make this pattern.
Write how many pegs in the pattern.

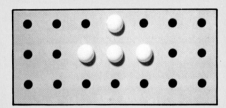

Add another row of pegs like this:
Write the number of pegs in
the pattern.
Continue the pattern adding a row
of pegs at a time.
Write the total number of pegs
in each pattern.

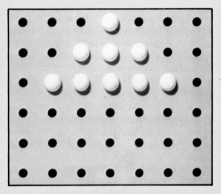

The numbers 1, 4, 9, 16, 25, . . .
are called **square numbers**.

You need a table square.
Colour in the square numbers.
What do you notice?

×	1	2	3	4	5	6	7	8	9	10
1	1	2	3	4	5	6	7	8	9	10
2	2	4	6	8	10	12	14	16	18	20
3	3	6	9	12	15	18	21	24	27	30
4	4	8	12	16	20	24	28	32	36	40
5	5	10	15	20	25	30	35	40	45	50
6	6	12	18	24	30	36	42	48	54	60
7	7	14	21	28	35	42	49	56	63	70
8	8	16	24	32	40	48	56	64	72	80
9	9	18	27	36	45	54	63	72	81	90
10	10	20	30	40	50	60	70	80	90	100

Make a number spiral
on squared paper.
Colour in the square
numbers.
What do you notice?

```
10-11-12-13
 9  2- 3 14
 8  1  4 15
 7- 6- 5 16
          17
```

5 squares, squared paper

Pentominoes

How many different shapes can you make using
5 squares?

Rules

1. The squares must fit side to side like this:

    You cannot have this:

    or this:

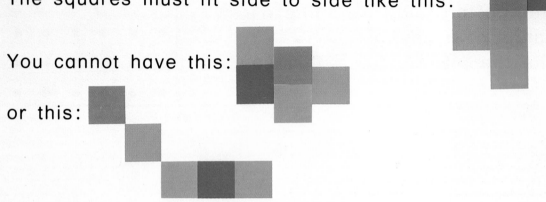

2. All the shapes must be different.

These shapes are really the same.
It is the same shape in a different position.

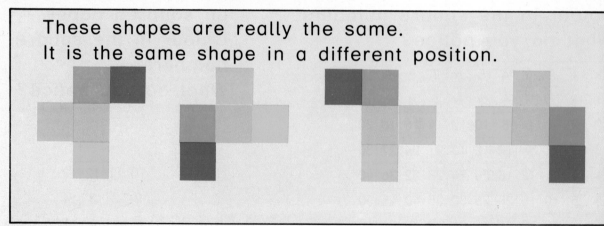

Now find all the different shapes you can using
5 squares.
Draw each shape on squared paper.
Each shape is called a pentomino.

Choose any one of your pentominoes.
Draw it again.
Cut it out.
Will it tessellate?
Will all the pentominoes tessellate?

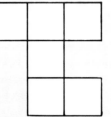

This is a hexomino.

It is made from 6 squares.
How many different hexominoes can you make?
Record your results on squared paper.

How many of your hexominoes
will fold to make a cube?

Problem Page

Peter has 5 clockwork cars.
He wound up each car and let it go.

Car number 1 travelled 19·40 m.
Car number 2 travelled 13·90 m.
Car number 3 travelled 12·50 m.
Car number 4 travelled 10·80 m.
Car number 5 travelled 7·90 m.

. Work out the distance between each car when they stopped.

. How far apart were the two cars which were closest when they stopped?

. How far was it from the first car to the last?

. How far would each car go if it was only half wound up?

. How far would each car go if it was fully wound up 5 times?

Addition and Subtraction – more practice

1.
```
  3647
   988
+ 1469
_____
```

2.
```
  4063
  1734
+   96
_____
```

3.
```
  1342
   737
+ 2862
_____
```

4.
```
   345
  1069
+ 2498
_____
```

5. Find the total of 1296, 27 and 480.

6. Add together 4016, 103, 978.

7. Increase 2741 by 2936.

8. Add 3729 to 986.

9.
```
  6317
- 4199
_____
```

10.
```
  2060
- 1379
_____
```

11.
```
  2948
- 1859
_____
```

12.
```
  6001
- 2973
_____
```

13. Find the difference between 1279 and 689.

14. How much greater than 2046 is 3097?

15. Subtract 979 from 2341.

16. From 3613 take 2874.

17. How much smaller than 2162 is 1874?

18. What number is 2146 less than 5000?

19. Find the difference between 4032 and 529.

20. How much greater than 1640 is 2893?

Multiplication and Division — more practice

1. 1036
    ×   3
    ____

2. 2047
    ×   4
    ____

3. 1492
    ×   6
    ____

4. 1139
    ×   7
    ____

5. 964
    ×   9
    ____

6. 1178
    ×   8
    ____

7. 1739
    ×   5
    ____

8. 1593
    ×   6
    ____

9. Multiply 874 by 10.

10. Which number is 8 times greater than 629?

11. $6\overline{)1242}$

12. $5\overline{)3790}$

13. $7\overline{)8436}$

14. $2\overline{)5260}$

15. $9\overline{)5729}$

16. $10\overline{)3729}$

17. $4\overline{)9216}$

18. $8\overline{)7265}$

19. $7\overline{)6108}$

20. Divide 7213 by 7.

21. Find $\frac{1}{8}$ of 7392.

22. Find $\frac{1}{4}$ of 6464.

23. What is $\frac{1}{3}$ of 3972?

Money — more practice

1. £
    1·37
    + 4·62
    ──────

    ──────

2. £
    0·93
    + 2·78
    ──────

    ──────

3. £
    7·46
    + 9·73
    ──────

    ──────

4. £
    8·07
    + 2·95
    ──────

    ──────

5. £
    3·93
    − 1·74
    ──────

    ──────

6. £
    6·28
    − 1·49
    ──────

    ──────

7. £
    3·09
    − 2·75
    ──────

    ──────

8. £
    6·00
    − 5·47
    ──────

    ──────

9. £
    1·68
    ×   9
    ──────

    ──────

10. £
    3·26
    ×   7
    ──────

    ──────

11. £
    0·76
    ×   8
    ──────

    ──────

12. £
    3·45
    ×   5
    ──────

    ──────

13. £

    6 ⟌ 9·24

14. £

    8 ⟌ 4·64

15. £

    7 ⟌ 11·34

16. £

    9 ⟌ 6·57

17. Find the total of £1·36, £4·87 and 39p.

18. What is the difference between £2·81 and £5·20?

19. Multiply £2·36 by 4.

20. Share £7·30 equally among 5 people.

68

Measurement — more practice

1.   m

     3·72

   + 7·59
   _____

2.   m

     2·08

   + 1·92
   _____

3.   m

     6·13

   − 2·74
   _____

4.   m

     2·31

   − 0·88
   _____

5. Find the total of 1·72 m, 2·39 m and 74 cm.

6. What is the difference between 1·72 m and 89 cm?

7. By how much is 2·79 m longer than 1·84 m?

8.   m

     1·72

   ×   8
   _____

9.   m

     0·83

   ×   9
   _____

10.   m

      2·74

    × 10
    _____

11.   m

      3·21

    ×   6
    _____

12.   m

    6) 9·42

13.   m

    7) 8·40

14.   m

    5) 3·90

15.   m

    9) 12·42

16. Multiply 3·72 m by 7.

17. Find $\frac{1}{2}$ of 9·36 m.

18. Find $\frac{1}{8}$ of 12·24 m.

19. Multiply 2·90 m by 9.

Assessment

1. Find the total of 2478, 49 and 3047.

2. £
   16·78
   + 9·84
   _____

3. m
   9·94
   + 5·85
   _____

4. £
   28·07
   − 19·18
   _____

5. m
   18·42
   − 8·94
   _____

6. Write the fraction coloured and not coloured.

7. $\frac{6}{8}$ is the same as $\square$

8. $9\overline{)4385}$

9. Find $\frac{1}{8}$ of £2·32.

10. Find the perimeter of this shape.

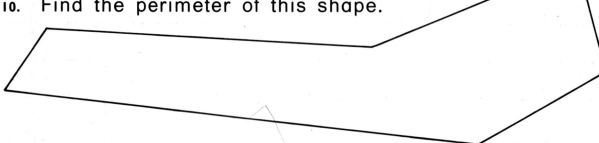

11. m
    5·72
    × 7
    _____

12. m
    $3\overline{)4·29}$

13. £
    8·46
    × 8
    _____

14.
    1238
    × 6
    _____

70

15. An _____ has three equal sides.

16.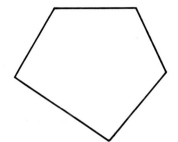

This shape is called
a _____ .

17.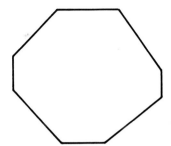

This shape is called
an _____ .

8. Draw round a circle and show a diameter.

9. Draw round a rectangle and show a diagonal.

0. Write the factors of 18.

1. What is the area of this shape?

2. Draw a graph showing the following information about people arriving at an airport.

Time	8·00–9·00	9·00–10·00	10·00–11·00	11·00–12·00
Number of people	350	600	550	400

Glossary

diagonal	a straight line joining two vertices
diameter	a straight line through the centre of a circle
digit	one of the numbers 0 to 9
equilateral triangle	a triangle with 3 equal sides
factor	the factors of 10 are 1, 2, 5 and 10
hexomino	a hexomino is made from 6 squares
kilogram (kg)	a measure of weight, 1000 g = 1 kg
millilitre (ml)	a measure of capacity, 1000 ml = 1 l
octagon	a shape with 8 straight sides
pentagon	a shape with 5 straight sides
pentomino	a pentomino is made from 5 squares
perimeter	the distance round a shape
quadrilateral	a shape with 4 straight sides
semi-circle	half a circle
tessellate	to fit shapes together without gaps
vertex	vertex
vertices	more than one vertex

72